WHAT DO WE KNOW ABOUT JUPITER?

ASTRONOMY BOOK FOR 6 YEAR OLDS

Children's Astronomy Books

BABY PROFESSOR

EDUCATION KIDS

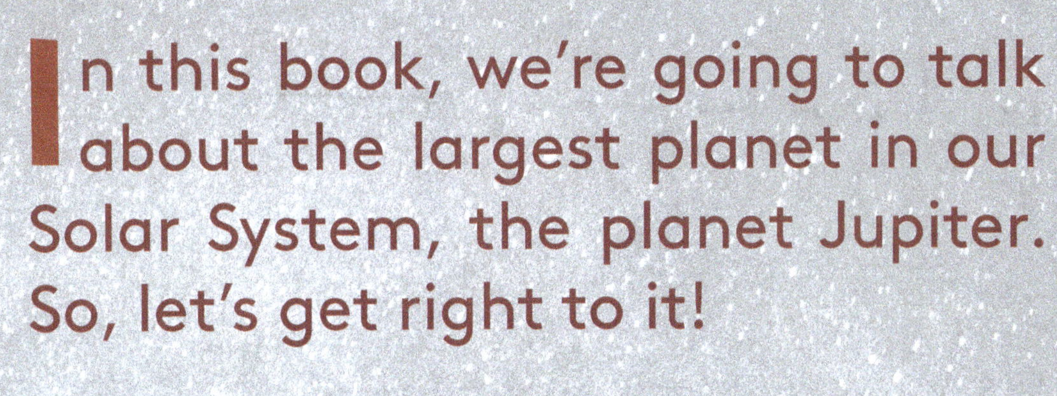

In this book, we're going to talk about the largest planet in our Solar System, the planet Jupiter. So, let's get right to it!

WHAT IS JUPITER?

Jupiter is a planet in our Solar System. Because it's so large, it was named Jupiter by the Romans and Zeus by the Greeks after the king of their gods. It's a perfect name for this planet since it's the largest in our Solar System. Of the eight planets, it's the fifth in distance from the Sun. This gas giant is an average of 484 million miles from the Sun.

GALILEO'S MOONS

When the Italian astronomer Galileo Galilei looked through his first telescope, he quickly discovered the four large moons of Jupiter. This important discovery in 1610 was another reason to believe that the Earth was in orbit around the Sun.

At that time, most people thought that the Earth was at the center of the universe. One hundred years before Galileo, in 1510, the Polish astronomer Nicolaus Copernicus had stated his theory that the Earth and other planets revolved around the Sun, but most people didn't believe this.

After all, the moon was revolving around our planet, so they thought we must be in the center. This was the first time that any other object in the sky was seen to have moons of its own too. Galileo was sure that the Earth and Jupiter were both planets that revolved around the Sun. He felt certain that Copernicus had been right. He named these four new moons, Ganymede, Callisto, Europa, and Io and they are known today as the Galilean satellites.

Ganymede is the largest moon in our Solar System. It's larger than the planet Mercury.

GANYMEDE

HOW BIG IS JUPITER?

If you were able to combine all the other planets in our Solar System, you would see that Jupiter is twice as massive as all of them put together. In terms of size, it's so big that you could put at least 1,200 of planet Earth inside it. Its mass is 318 times the mass of Earth.

If it was 80 times its current size, then instead of forming into a planet, it would have formed into a star. Its atmosphere is made up of the same elements as the Sun is made of, hydrogen and helium. This is why Jupiter is called a gas giant.

The four moons that Galileo saw in this telescope weren't the only ones circling Jupiter. We now know that Jupiter has at least 60 moons!

So many bodies are in orbit around Jupiter that it's like having a Solar System with a planet at its center.

COLORFUL BANDS AND DIAMOND RAIN

If you looked at Jupiter in a telescope, you would see that it has different horizontal bands of colors. Some of the bands are dark in color and some are lighter. The colors in the bands are caused by chemicals.

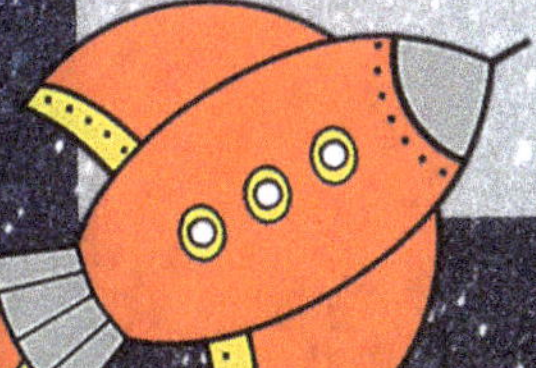

Jupiter has very strong winds that travel from east to west at over 400 miles per hour! These bands don't stay the same in size, but instead change over time. Scientists think that deep down in Jupiter's atmosphere there could be liquid diamonds that rain down like water does on Earth. You couldn't stand on the surface of Jupiter because it has a surface made of gas.

THE GREAT RED SPOT

On Earth we have large hurricanes that cause a lot of destruction, but we don't have any storms as large as the storms on Jupiter. Jupiter has a strange red spot that astronomers have seen for over 300 years. At its widest point, the Great Red Spot has a diameter that's three times the size of Earth's diameter.

he storm is spinning at a rate of 225 miles per hour. Scientists believe its color comes from chemicals that compose the storm. The Great Red Spot isn't always the same size and in recent years it's gotten smaller. Once in a while it almost fades away. We still have a lot to learn about this mysterious storm.

JUPITER'S MAGNETIC FIELD

Earth has a magnetic field and Jupiter does too. Its magnetic field has a force that's 20,000 times Earth's strength. The level of radiation around its rings and moons would be lethal to human beings.

he radiation field travels out millions of miles around the planet. This field of electrically charged particles is called Jupiter's magnetosphere. It stretches out about 2 million miles between Jupiter and the Sun and extends behind the planet for over 600 million miles.

DAYS AND YEARS ON JUPITER

Jupiter spins more rapidly than any of the other planets. It has a full day in about 9.8 hours compared to the Earth's day in 24 hours. Its one year is equivalent to about 11.9 Earth years.

COMPOSITION AND STRUCTURE

The atmosphere on Jupiter is about 90% hydrogen and 10% helium. The remaining 10% is other gases like ammonia and methane. It's essentially a gigantic ball of gases.

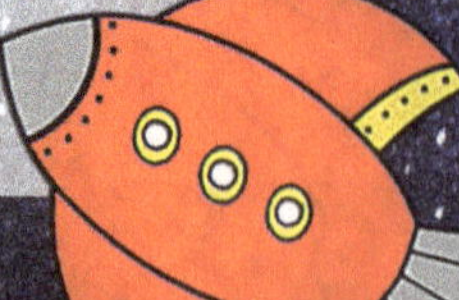

Scientists are not sure of the exact composition of Jupiter's core. They do know that its core is about 10 times the mass of the Earth.

It's wrapped in a fluid form of hydrogen that extends out from the core to about 80% of the planet's diameter. The average temperature on the planet's surface is minus 234 degrees Fahrenheit.

ORBIT AND ROTATION

Just like all the other planets, Jupiter's distance from the Sun varies at different times. When it's the closest to the Sun, it's 460,276,100 miles away. When it's farthest from the Sun it's 507,089,500 miles away.

THE MOONS OF JUPITER

Jupiter has lots of moons—63 and counting!

Ganymede is the largest and it's even larger than the planet Mercury and the dwarf planet Pluto. It's the only moon in our Solar System that has a magnetic field of its own. It also has an ocean although it's wedged between thick blocks of ice.

Io has tons of volcanoes. Its volcanic activity spews out a lot of sulfur, which gives it a blotchy appearance of yellow and orange. The gravitational pull of Jupiter causes Io's surface to rise in 300-foot waves of towering and collapsing mountains just like water rises and falls in waves on Earth. This makes Io's volcanoes even more active.

Europa's crust is largely made of ice. Astronomers think that under the ice there may be a huge liquid ocean with twice the amount of water held by Earth's oceans. There's a possibility that oceans may exist on Ganymede and Callisto too. Future missions to Europa will be needed to find out more since Europa might have life or become a place for life to exist.

Callisto is the least shiny of any of the larger moons. Astronomers believe that its surface is made of rock.

THE RINGS OF JUPITER

Astronomers thought that Saturn was the only planet in our Solar System to have rings but Jupiter has three rings too. The Voyager 1 spacecraft found them in 1979. They are not as visible as Saturn's rings.

The main ring is flat and its thickness is about 20 miles. The halo, which is the inner ring, is about 12,000 miles in thickness. It expands and contracts according to the planet's magnetic activity. Both of these rings are made up of tiny particles.

The third ring is called the gossamer ring because it's kind of see-through. It's made up of dust with particles the size of cigarette smoke. The rings have ripples in them and astronomers believe that these ripples were formed when they were hit by asteroids or comets.

RESEARCH AND EXPLORATION

There have been eight missions by unmanned spacecraft that have either flown by or orbited the giant planet. Pioneer 10 and 11 were the earliest, followed by Voyager 1 and 2.

The Pioneer spacecraft discovered the dangers of Jupiter's radiation and provided more information on the Red Spot. Its four largest moons were researched by Voyager as well as its rings. The Ulysses mission provided information on how the Sun's solar wind affects Jupiter and the New Horizons mission took close-up snapshots of the planet.

In 1995, the Galileo mission was crashed into Jupiter on purpose so that it would not crash into Europa. Its mission was to measure

the planet's atmosphere. The Juno mission is in progress as of 2016 and will yield more information about this amazing planet.

GRAVITATIONAL IMPACT

The huge gravitational pull of Jupiter has had an impact on how the Solar System was shaped. It's believed that Jupiter had an effect on how far Neptune and Uranus are from the Sun at the time the Solar System was forming. When they were forming they got hurled out from the center just like rocks from a slingshot.

COULD THERE BE ANY LIFE ON JUPITER?

Even though there's no evidence of life on Jupiter, it doesn't mean that there is none there. Scientists believe that if you were able to travel past the beginning layer of icy atmosphere, that the temperature gets warmer. In those warmer temperatures of about 70 degrees Fahrenheit some organisms that live in air could exist.

Awesome! Now you know more about the planet Jupiter. You can find more Astronomy books from Baby Professor by searching the website of your favorite book retailer.

Visit
BABY PROFESSOR
EDUCATION KIDS
www.BabyProfessorBooks.com
to download Free Baby Professor eBooks
and view our catalog of new and exciting
Children's Books